Losing Touch

Andrew Leggett

Losing Touch

Acknowledgements

Most of these poems saw first publication in the following journals: *Bareknuckle Poet* (Australia), *Blue Pepper Poetry* (Australia), *Burrow* (Australia), *Children, Churches and Daddies* (USA), *Cordite Poetry Journal (Australia), e.ratio Poetry Journal (USA), Eunoia Review* (Singapore), *foam:e* (Australia), *Folded Word* (USA), *Ginosko Literary Journal* (USA), *Quadrant* (Australia), *Small Packages* (Australia), *Social Alternatives* (Australia), *StylusLit* (Australia), *Stylus Poetry Journal* (Australia), *Survision Magazine* (Ireland), *Text Journal* (Australia), *The Blue Nib* (Ireland), *The Canberra Time*s (Australia), *Weber – the Contemporary West* (USA), *The Weekend Australian* (Australia), *When Anzac Day Comes Around: Gallipoli 100 Years Poetry Anthology* (Australia), *Wild Musette* (USA).

'Frogmouth Blood Moon Blues', 'Jazz Show in the Vines' and 'Listening to Lead Belly' have been recorded as song lyrics, on the Blood Moon label, by the Blood Moon Wailers.

In an earlier draft, 'Watching the Bridge' was shortlisted for the Gwen Harwood Poetry Prize (Australia).

'Mother of Pearl' was shortlisted for the Bridport Poetry Prize (UK).

'Reverie', 'Arm' and 'Window' made the long list for the Joanne Burns Microlit Award (Australia).

Losing Touch
ISBN 978 1 76109 246 6
Copyright © text Andrew Leggett 2022

First published 2022 by
GINNINDERRA PRESS
PO Box 3461 Port Adelaide 5015
www.ginninderrapress.com.au

Contents

Losing Touch	7
Playhouse Theatre	9
I Held a Flame	10
Shadow	11
Milton to Katherine	12
Alila Fever, Ubud	13
Chorten	14
Two Wrasse and a Yellow-fin Bream	16
Great Notion Road	17
Watching the Bridge	20
Film Noir Dreaming	22
Pulped Fiction	23
Smoking Gun	24
Lazarus	26
Stones	28
Merengue in Purgatory	29
Mother of Pearl	30
Fisherman's Wife	31
Bird	33
I Must Swim	34
Push Me	35
Terminus	37
Downpipe	38
Silence and the Rose	39
Old Hat	40
Camera Obscura	42
Sax For Sale	43
Listening to Lead Belly	44
Where Oil Drums Go To Die	45
Kyushu Airman, 1945	46

ANZACS at the Bar	47
Simpson and His Donkey, 1915	48
Iron Lung	49
For Joseph Coleman, 1810–1833	50
Breaking the Pane	51
My Father Came Back	52
Reverie	53
Arm	54
Window	55
Limb	56
Sheen	57
Small Change	58
1831 Boutique Hotel	59
Boomer Stew	60
After the Rain	61
Magenta Shores	62
Jazz Show in the Vines	64
Benedictine On Ice	65
Frogmouth Blood Moon Blues	68
My Familiar Frogmouth	69
Leaving	74
About the Author	75

Losing Touch

We have left you to move out
along the coast that divides
this land of citizens
from the leviathan depths,
where the whale's cry bounces
and echoes down trenches,
mourning its lost calf,
and the tiger shark lusts
for the board rider
on her trajectory across the face
between crest and trough,
bloody dreams disrupted
when both shark and surfer
pull out before the breakers
crash in over the rocks.

As we proceed
down the Pacific Highway
in our solitary vehicle
packed with suitcases
and the casket for my old guitar,
the removalists travel separately.
There are no floral tributes
or cortege to follow us,
through scars of fire and flood,
across the boundaries set
by the urban weekend magazine.

You may not recognise us
when we rendezvous again
at a bohemian music festival
or wine tasting at some limestone
vineyard, where you might
see through us as phantoms
thrown up by the *kairos*
of sea spray that surrounds us,
ethereally thin as we've become,
having lost the knotted tongues
with which we once conversed
on the pratfalls and the merits
of contemporary cinema.

Playhouse Theatre

When we go to the theatre
in the midst of the languor
of age and decrepitude
I want you to be wearing
your high-heeled slingbacks
a black backless frock
with a plunging halter
and that choker of pearls
you stole from your mother
for a secret liaison
with a crushed hibiscus
lewd as the mangroves
when the tide recedes
under art's concrete bunker.

I Held a Flame

Just for a while, you said.
Until I return.
        I waited,
hoping, when you came back,
you would hold a flame
for me too,

that we would go walking
through a stand of eucalypts
with the underbrush tinder-dry,
our flames for each other
setting the forest ablaze,
flaring incandescent
against the night sky.

Then the rain came.
I stood out in the storm,
holding my flame for you
under a beach umbrella,
hoping, when you came back,
we could sunbake nude,
then plunge together
into the pool of tears I shed.

Shadow

My hairdresser's eyes
were delicate windows
with awnings shadowed
in fluorescent aqua
and fringed with lashes
of kohl-black mascara.
I told her of fever
that burned in the seventies
for girls in the city
with blue eye shadow.
Their acrylic-tipped fingers
wore an itch to scratch
less tender than hers
as she worked at the basin.

After the fire
that burned out the salon
my hairdresser's eyes
were blackened windows
to a shut-down soul
still open for business
but closed to kindness.
I raked the embers
until I found words
to bring on grief's labour
in a basin of tears.
I have forgotten her name
but I won't forget the colour
of my hairdresser's eyes.

Milton to Katherine

I can no longer look into your eyes.
Will you guide me as the sun fades
the sky to indigo through seven shades
of blue? And will the stars caress your thighs
when I have come to realise I've failed?
Reach through the veil to take my hand
and lead this poet, Kate, to understand
the planet Venus glows when day has failed;
that night is good for lovers who depend
on other senses to remove brocade,
unfasten stays and play at masquerade.
Such gentle games do more than time to mend
the cruel tears. They prematurely end.
Our child is born. My lover is a shade.

Alila Fever, Ubud

path between rice fields
lined with stone lanterns
bears the hotel's new name

fourteen years past
our bed in the chedi
we check in again

wayan in uniform
son of the old staff
sprays insects at dusk

japanese nymph wraiths
float with the mist
on the infinity pool

pining for tennyo
long since the yen failed
my desire remains strong

seven steps down
to the sandstone shrine
with an empty throne

our dreams rise as dust
departing the alila
when fever has passed

Chorten

On the ridge that divides
the Imja Valley from the Khumbu
stands a cluster of chortens:
stone upon stone,
one formed of two towers,
a bridge between piles
and a capstone,
with a secondary tower
on the Dingboche side.

Djungbu, my guide,
has summited Everest
fourteen times.

I ask, 'Are these stones
memorials
for those who have died?'

Djungbu replies, 'People come.
They build,
remember many lives.'

The jet stream ripples
a wisp of cloud
as it roars over Lohtse.

I point my camera
at the black ice wall
holding the lake
on Ama Dablam.

Ravens ride the thermals
up the ridge from Periche.

When the sun burns the wall
The village will drown.

Two Wrasse and a Yellow-fin Bream

I cast my lure into the confusion
of foam strewn up in the wake
of the launch departing Tangalooma pier.
This piece of speckled orange polyurethane
spins, trailing a pair of barbed tridents,
belly-and-tail-rigged.
I wind the ratchet-set reel
Jarvis Walker made for me in China,
land the fish and, in the thrash of spines,
relent of filleting its life. I rush
to dislodge the hooks and throw its dying form
through seas of air. The splash disturbs Japan,
whose citizens stand behind me, bent over
a bucket of two wrasse, caught unawares.

Great Notion Road

God is in Heaven. The fish in the tank
in the Thai restaurant, Exhibition Street, Melbourne,
will never see stars fall.

Neil Armstrong rocketed a quarter
million miles to the moon,
a long trip for a small step.

A sign beyond Westgate Bridge
marks our slow progress under the sun
one kilometre from Ceres. Armstrong is dead.

Let us debate who first saw the lighthouse
come over the rise at Split Point.
Wild horses of cloud ride the sky.

Where the sun dips, I fell behind
the retinue on that ridge above Fairhaven.
I will look to the east for your return.

From Erskine Falls to Teddy's Lookout.
above the St George River Estuary,
voices tumbling over stones mouth clichés of beauty.

The road is sinuous as the sigmoid colon,
continuous to Apollo Bay. Ocean to port,
land starboard. No Apollo splashdown.

Not Armstrong, not Aldrin, nor Collins would pay
to enter the lighthouse at Cape Otway,
so they circle the Bight in spiral orbit.

There were Twelve Apostles. Only nine remain.
Peter, Andrew, Mark, Matthew, Luke, Nathaniel,
Judas, James and John signal the astronauts over the bay.

There are no astronauts, but the angels came down
through a gap in the clouds, just beyond
the limestone pillars, an excellent home for birds.

That fish in the tank knows nothing of wind farms,
nor of sheep on the road to Mount Gambier.
It may bang on the glass, but never will walk on the moon.

The lighthouse at Robe is of modern design:
three concrete slabs with a globe
in a cyclone and barbed wire enclosure.

The fibreglass lobster claws at the sky
from the roadside café at Kingston,
the first crustacean beyond Port Fairy.

When the fish left its tank, Armstrong rose up
and the crayfish broke free from its moorings.
They tyrannised sheep by the salt pans of Coorong.

Armstrong to Aldrin: 'Buzz, on the moon,
there were no wind farms, no lighthouses,
no fibreglass crayfish.' 'Desolate!' says Aldrin.

Across the causeway on Victor Harbor,
we walk by moonlight around Granite Island.
I was alone when I saw the rainbow.

As the ferry docks at Penneshaw,
a fur seal flicks its whiskers. Silver cars
slip down the ramp like pilchards.

From Kingscote to Seal Bay,
red earth and grey-green scrub,
divided by tarmac from fields of canola.

On the ironstone road to the Marron Café
there are no fibreglass crayfish. The marron
in the tanks go well with chardonnay.

If God was an astronaut, what would She say
to the Cape du Couedic seals at play in the cove
and all the marsupials killed on the road

back to Kingscote at dusk? Wallabies burst
out of the scrub, bound back and forth
in the path of the car, into the scrub again.

The road from the Cape Jervis ferry
branches left to Adelaide, sinuous
along the valley to Yankalilla Bay.

On the Florieau, ghost gums and lavender farms,
roan Angus beasts and black-faced lambs,
all toast on the way, under the sun.

On long hauls through space, do astronauts dream
of summer love, or crayfish with fibreglass claws?
Ask the fish in the tank! Armstrong is silent.

Watching the Bridge

A smudge on the line
between bridge and sky,
another semi-trailer thunders.

Light breaks the storm.
Each end of the bridge
is the start of a rainbow.

No one looks at the hill
where the dead lie,
in the midfield of vision.

Swaying eucalypts whisper
names razed from stones
in the garden of immanence.

Lorikeets fight a single finch
over nectar in the stellate flowers
of the umbrella.

This humid afternoon
sheds its musty kimono.
I stand and shiver

in my black speedos,
inspecting bonsai
in a tub of pebbles.

It has rained
on the crush of lilies
sprayed with citronella.

A puddle dries,
exposing fossil ferns.
Evolution slows during peak hour.

In a storm,
when I am gone,
another semi-trailer thunders.

No shag on the hunt,
nor squid's eye in the bay,
could capture this on film.

Film Noir Dreaming

Along the boundary, worlds collide in regions of discontinuity
into which I slip through curiosity, lured by traces patients confide.
This weight of information makes me long for the confessional,
but I cannot shed this professional burden of fiduciary obligation.

These dreams, of sunbursts peeking out above the seams,
overflow in dam bursts, an imbroglio of swollen breasts
leaping from their *balconnets*. Strange desires, ephemeral
as flatterers of lewd suits, flare and flicker their little fires.

And yet I dream of a marathon carnival for which I train
too hard in the heat, too long on the road, with no recovery,
so much so that, at the pre-race urinal, I stream the colour
of a cabernet, dolorous the schedule, harbinger of the terminal.

I'd rather dream of a raven woman, with lips the colour
of cherry-red patent leather, mouthing: 'I am the morello!'
in the tunnel of fear, where the drum of the heart beats hollow
and hands run on the silk-seamed calves of the femme fatale.

Pulped Fiction

Nigel Carruthers lay in a white porcelain clawfoot bath; his feet secured with plastic zip ties; his arms pinioned fast behind his back. The wild bacillus scent of unpasteurised goat's milk tantalised his nostrils as the nutriment soaked the weave of his cashmere morning suit and lapped at the cleft of his impudent chin. He had often anticipated his wedding night, but never had he dreamed of this. His horned bride knelt beside the tub; collar of her black cat suit upturned; the zip itself unfurled to the waist, allowing her freedom to express fluid from the cherry tips of her fecund breasts. Her freshly hennaed hair hung down her back. From Nigel's viewpoint, though, it was pulled back around the roots of her caprine tines by a jewelled tiara, tight enough to show her widow's peak. Above her head, a sole naked globe, suspended from the ceiling on a frayed maroon cloth chord, cast shadows on his smooth shaven skin. She reached into the bath to retrieve a sodden book, then tore, one by one, only the solicited pages of *Pulped Fiction*, scrunched them into balls and thrust them mercilessly down Nigel's grateful throat.

Smoking Gun

Spreading on the mattress
of a nicotine deckchair,
Hemingway's clone raises a lighter
to a stub of Havana cigar,
catching the eye of my Canon Legria,
snapped with the legs
of his sexagenarian blonde
companion sticking out
in the lower right-hand
corner of the frame.

Given a push,
with timed exposure
and a tumble on the path,
the snap of the legs
at the greater trochanter,
caught by the magnetic
resonance image scanner,
gives a surgeon joy.

Racked retractors
make the way for the jigsaw.
The whining blade bites bone,
spattering the face mask
like the head in the brush chipper
in that scene from *Fargo*.

The surgeon perks
as the old arthritic hip gives way,
wielding his ceramic ball
in its titanium socket.

With a couple of bangs
as sharp as Christ on nails
with a sock around the throat,
soon the old man will spray
and dance the cancan,
if I delay the shutter speed
and he keeps right on puffing.

Steady now,
his belly rises,
portside out,
starboard home,
rocking on a makeshift raft
with a Galapagos tortoise
blowing the sail with a bellows.

I squat, peer into this snapshot,
then tap a sniper's view
into the keyboard, mind's eye
raising steel to my shoulder.
Plugged between his dentures,
the stub of that flaming stoogie
positions in the crosshairs
of my infrared sights.

Lazarus

Few men who stink as I do
have been pursued by poetry,

whether the muse be chimera, sphinx,
or other distortion of the great cat.

Why must I be the kill to whom
she returns at the end of her prowl?

Fresh from the sepulchre,
mine are as fleet as any athlete's feet.

I rise, reeking of tinea and sweat
less fragrant than vanilla

since my sweet sister poured the myrrh
I missed all over Jesus' feet.

Yes, I am up for it, stretching
at the door of the tomb at dawn,

ready to break into a run before
poetry springs to maul me again.

Last night I dreamed of slow recovery
from injuries inflicted by the beast.

I found myself bandaged
in a military hospital. All I could do

was swing my plastered limb
wildly to starboard as my good arm

tugged at the triangle on the iron cot
at the nightingale end of the ward.

Our Lady Phosphorescent
cast candle light into the hollows

where once there were my eyes.
With no defence to mount,

I tossed a glass of atomised sago
into my tangle of sheets

and promised weeping Jesus never
to give up the struggle to rise.

Stones

The breakers rise and crest,
then roar across the shelf,
scattering small stones
across the beach. I search
among them, reach
for the first black oval,
raise it to the sky,
dark opacity
against the blue.

I need to hold
tight to the earth.
I spot another, russet brown
against the sand,
grasp it in my hand,
stack it, red against black.

Topped with a third
small piece of greenstone,
I balance them
as a cairn –
green, brown, black –
down from the mountain,
rolled in the river,
my gift to you
the sea brought back.

Merengue in Purgatory

for Gwen Harwood

Along the shore, where waves of the unborn
tear up the scree and clinker of the dead
the poet skips across the foam in red
pumps Fiorelli made too steep to be worn
outside the bedroom. Eisenbart exhumes
himself to caper beside her on cloven hooves
as dressed by Dante, the man with the moves
from *Dancing With the Stars.* He snorts and fumes
as Petrarch pats his shoulder, cutting in
on this last dance with his creator, Gwen.
He tucks his tail and slinks off to his den
to sulk at the machismo butting in
while Petrarch holds her tight, and quite the flirt
pats her rump and flicks at her lambada skirt.

Mother of Pearl

When you left the beach
to tend the threat
of your father's failing heart
I walked the twins to Gelatissimo.

A blonde girl with outgrowth
the colour of her boxer's coat
left the dog tied to a pole
while she sought hazelnut and pistacchio.

Once served, she bent so low the dog
licked cream from her cheeks
and the jagged hem of her denim skirt
tore my chest apart.

The little girls chose lemon and maroon
confectionery in cups
before we crossed the road
to the tidal pools

where mother plunged
as a lamina of chrome
into the helix.

Fisherman's Wife

for Talib Odeh

Stolen from the sea,
her torso sways to the right,
then snakes to the left again.

A woman without arms
moves to the oud,
to the beat of the tabla.

She is woman below,
but above the waist,
she is all fish.

Up and down her spine,
from the tip of her tail
to the jewel in her crown,
moves a tube of light.

She snatches at air
like a bellows hungry
for the ocean to blow
in and out of her gills.

Her belly rises
below the line
where scales meet skin,

all the way down
to that silken place
where he will taste fish.

When she grows fins
she will swim far away from him
and be free in the ocean again.

Bird

A bird lands on the jacaranda
below the terrace,
feeds and flies away
to the soughing eucalypt.

With the breeze,
the mesh of the trellis
wavers and bends.

Nasturtiums regenerate
faster than honeysuckle,
striving to pull down
the afternoon sun.

That bird has not returned
but another warbles somewhere.

I Must Swim

A ukulele tinkles,
softer than a mandolin.
Then strains break.

I thought you were gone,
but you are behind me,
strumming and singing.

Your heat is at my shoulder
as you pray on the strings
and raise your song.

I disregard the instrument,
but as you lay it down
and unzip your skirt,

you plunge into the ocean
of my thoughts. I am drawn
to the thigh line of your one-piece.

You break the surface
of my pool of reverie
and I must swim.

Push Me

Following a locum doctor,
your days are spent
in and out of a suitcase.

Our motel room
gives way to breakfast
snatched from the window
of a fast food drive through.

All day I tend flowers
and pull out weeds
from mental gardens.

Sundown finds me
alone in the office,
making a record entry.

You park in the drive,
then pace as I type furiously.

It's late on this dark street,
among figs with no birds
and withering jacarandas.

These records and a pane of glass
keep me from your kiss.

I enter my electronic signature,
code the alarm,
lock the door and step out.

Drive me to the aquatic centre.
Let the shock of blue chlorine
wash histories from my skin.

Drive me to the pool
and push me in.

Terminus

Rain beats on the helipad –
just a surgical floor between us
and the Medivac dropping organs
for the transplant team.
The chopper hovers
before heading back
over Indooroopilly Island
where a cacophony of bats
belts out a symphony.

Under the shudder
of receding wings
we contemplate
your heart's last beat.
No parcel bears your name.
There is no matching donor.
Gratuitous condolences
rush from my throat
like hornets.

Downpipe

From my office window, through the vertical slats of the blind, the space I see could be a prison yard. There is no escape from the stone wall of the high dependency unit. It bears a crooked downpipe, bent and discontinuous at shoulder height where rust shows through, at the broken joint, below the russet paint. The iron roof curves away above the guttering to form a stark horizon where it meets the cyan sky, across which wisps of stratus cloud drift, occasionally crossing the half a ball that makes the day's first quarter moon. This is not a day for rain, so the spider in the broken pipe not will be evicted. Patients may be discharged, but spider remains.

Silence and the Rose

This afternoon, silence on the drive is welcome. Music plays on Spotify, but I remember silence. Sometimes memories are welcome. At the hospital, I am surprised by a rose garden. As I make my way, up car park levels, via stairs and elevators, passing gantries, to the right place, I know that I will find my students. They wait for me, holding case notes, tight as sprinters on starting blocks hold their heartbeats for the gun. I am glad to find among them an idealist and an optimist. After the tutorial, I remember the garden at the bottom of the steps to my own old school. I am young again. I bend to steal a rose.

Old Hat

Rainbow lorikeets and mynas feast
on palm flower nectar and the red stellate flowers
of the umbrella. I turn from the window,
rise from my desk, pack my notebook,
my laptop, mobile phone, wallet,
half-devoured tubs of hummus and taramasalata,
an intact packet of brown rice crackers
and a pinot gris in a lime green cooler.
I reach for my panama hat, a white fedora,
softened with sweat, with salt lines on the band
and blood stains on the crown no number of runs
through the dishwasher will ever render clean,
those well above the rent in the brim
where the fibres have begun to move
towards their own unraveling.

My old hat and I are driving across town
to a meeting in a tall apartment building
just across the street from the hospital
where my friend died last night, a couple of hours
after we left her. From the living room
the view of the old brown river is good.
On the day they drained her pericardial effusion,
the river was rising, just about to burst
its banks. The rain was lashing me and the wind
was so strong that I almost lost my umbrella.
Along the covered way between the buildings,
plastic buckets kept the drips from the carpet.

When I enter the room, I am informed
of the decision for White Lady Funerals,
their rooms just streets away from my place,
at Seven Hills, near Morningside. Those ladies
buried my Aunt, took her frail body to Hemmant
from Cannon Hill and never brought it back.
I lift my hat and place it on the table.
I will not throw it in the ring, where the widower
deliberates between burial and cremation,
mentions the virtues of a plot on multiple levels –
one for her, one for him, and one for their girl,
who plays with her iPad and is not dead yet.

I open the crackers, distribute the wine –
the body and the blood. I've brought the only food.
I wish I'd stopped to purchase loaves and fishes.
I am assigned the music task, all on account
of my vast collection of Leonard Cohen.
I agree to help collect the coffin, flown in
from New Zealand, strapped to the roof
of a Volkswagen, and driven across town
to be customised. I offer to feed them all
at the wake before the wake
for my friend who will never wake again
at my place next Sunday. I collect
my computer, my notebook, the lime-green cooler
and leave to shop at Woolworths,
wearing my old panama hat.

Camera Obscura

Bereft, Prince Leo Nikolayevich
Myshkin, last and poorest of a line
of blue-eyed optimists, sits on a bench
alone and waits for a blonde woman in boots
to appear in the shadows of his autumn wish,
to only say the word and you'll be mine.
He gives his bottle a rub. No genie. No wench.
No chorus of derision. The screeches and the hoots
ring out as accolades from teen coquettes
playing in the park. Their pleas for cigarettes
make him laugh out loud as he retreats
from riding the roundabout of *jeune fillettes,*
bumps into a secret door in the walled rotunda
and falls, never to emerge from the camera obscura.

Sax For Sale

Passing the pawn shop, I am drawn
to the Conn saxophone in the window display,
tagged at just over a grand
but cash in hand could be had
for a grand, with a price drop,
or laid by with three months to pay –
a long wait before bebop
shawahwah.
                Why, brother
did you sell your soul
did you sell your horn
your tenor sax?

You could not save your soul.
You would not hold your seed.
There were no oats to sow.
She would not have you
have your way. You could not
be the man with the horn.
She would not let you blow.
You would not blow her way.

Listening to Lead Belly

Home from the Boundary, after the Delta Crowes,
turning on Lead Belly on the Rock Island Line
at twenty to midnight, I'm praying to snatch
fragments of meaning to ride into the light
that Lead Belly saw flash across the cell wall,
with freedom the hope of sharing a boxcar.

Crossing the boundaries with easy kisses,
bridging the distance of a walk in silence,
chewin' cracked corn, covered in cotton bolls
from head to toe, we ride into the light
that Lead Belly saw flash across the cell wall,
with freedom the hope of sharing a boxcar.

I'm humming and strumming from treble to bass
on an old guitar in a place that knows love,
no love no more. Oh lordy, lord knows,
who knows what love is? Ride into the light
that Lead Belly saw flash across the cell wall,
with freedom the hope of sharing a boxcar.

But lord I know, Lead Belly tells me one thing I know.
I'm listening, Lead Belly. You tell me sweet kisses
break across the rhythm of chain gang hammers
bashing to shatter this fragile belly of love.

Where Oil Drums Go To Die

In the land where oil drums go to die
lived jazz cornetist Papa Mutt Carey,
who raised his horn and blew 'Get Out of Here
(And Go On Home)', waking memories of 1944
and a creole band with trombone man Kid Ory.

The drums, some stacked in lines, some sprawling
on the grass, beat back a Melanesian story
of past lives served as makeshift rafts
bearing soldiers in jungle greens,
drifting in the Coral Sea without a radio,
praying for the navy as the storms rolled in.

Kyushu Airman, 1945

for Teddy J. Ponzcka

Softly and quietly then, when the airman fell,
there was no sound, just a susurration of the air
savoured by the villagers for the tumult
of its vibration against the blade of a spear
penetrating the alien chest,
which bled starlight then,
as might the Nephilim.

Serum clear as truth but slight as science
oozed from many underbelly wounds inflicted
by desire of those who sought to bring him down.
Consensus and deference prevailed, so this aviator,
trusting the beneficence of medical men,
found himself, on waking,
plundered, eviscerated,
                      and imminently dead.

ANZACS at the Bar

I will raise you a flute of my fierce loving kindness,
if you bring home Charley and Frank, Ahmet and Mehmet,
rather than choke on a yard glass of tears of my enemies,

drained from the dunes where they fell to their knees
to pray from the shoulder, an Enfield, a Mauser, a hit.
I will raise you a flute of my fierce loving kindness.

Be it 'Crikey!' or '*Tanri uludur*!" they cry in your likeness
as that shell from Mal Tepe takes another cadet
and I choke on the yard glass of tears of my enemies.

Young men fresh from the farm crossed wild seas
to doubt the right that spurts from the bayonet.
I'll raise you a flute of my fierce loving kindness.

Dead men, blown in the grime of Empire's blindness,
cocoon shrapnel, like seeds in a pomegranate,
rather than choke on a yard glass of tears of my enemies.

To the gods Frank and Charley died to appease,
to Ahmet, to Mehmet! Pour them a sherbert.
I will raise you a flute of my fierce loving kindness,
rather than choke on a yard glass of tears of my enemies.

Simpson and His Donkey, 1915

As I pace the memorial
late in November,
distracted from revision
of a writerly paper,
mythology brays at me
from a gauche statue.

Children wired poppies
into the bridle
of the bronze donkey,
where they remain
from Remembrance Day.

Side saddle,
the wounded digger
keeps his slouch
as a shell burst
shrapnels his chest.

Simpson's blind.
The intelligent eyes
are those of the donkey.
Why, oh why,
must the ass die?

Iron Lung

for Roy Richard Gray, 1922–1953

It's been a long day at the mill and I'm tired,
but I think of the kids and swallow my pride.
I pull off my boots. Feet are needles and pins.
My low back aches and my ribs are lead.
Something's not right, but I let it slide.
I'm feverish as I lie by your side

I wake in the night with a throbbing head.
My neck is stiff and I can't move my legs.
The walls are too close and dark's closing in.
The air seems foul and I struggle to breathe.
I retch and I'm sick all over the sheets.
I cause you to wake to my shame and my dread.

It's a two hour drive to the hospital.
You shake with tears at the wheel.
I struggle to breathe by your side
and I'm overcome by fear.
When the doctor says it's polio,
into the iron lung I slide.

For Joseph Coleman, 1810–1833

As the sun goes behind the hill above Glebe Gully,
I think of you, Joseph and wonder, where did you go,
after they hanged you by the neck at Old Banks
on the Paterson River? Are you here, at Maitland,
under this ground, where they dumped the remains
of convicts in anonymous holes – no more dishonour
for you than Greenway, the forger, whose best
designs would not spare this plot, where he came
through cholera, five years after you? He dissolved
in your mould, that of you and your neighbours,
whose bones were scattered and mingled with others
as earth shifted with the Hunter's quakes and floods.
Whether your bones lie in this ground, or not,
has your spirit flown past the sun, back to London?

Did your brother know? Did Townshend send Henry
from Gresford that day, to stand with the chaplain
and ask would he write something home to your mother?
Did Henry speak regret for the way he taught you
to pick a gent's pocket and he'd always remember
you held him and fed him when taken with fever
during the lay-up when the ship drove to Spithead
before that long journey on the *Marquis of Huntley*?
Did they send Edward Cory to let you say sorry
you lifted that shovel to strike his head and to pray
for forgiveness, (though I've read that you said
you'd sooner hang than work for him another day)?
And when it was done and you were dead, did
Henry's tears wash before they took you away?

Breaking the Pane

Down in the hole
under the ground
no access to matches
Father is locked
safe in his box.
If I had a hammer
I'd smash the glass
sound the alarm
reach for the fire.

My Father Came Back

My father came back from the grave.
He broke his silence with an unknowing look.
He said, 'Son, you're old and bald and fat.'
'Thanks, Dad! You're not at your best.
Those eighteen years under the hill
have not treated you kindly,' was all I said.
He did not take umbrage. There was no fight
in him. He had become the kind of spook
I could poke right through, like a hole in my hat.
'To have become like you, is that so bad?'
With no comfort to offer, without a sound,
he withdrew from the mirror, back underground.

Reverie

Staring through the mesh screen that separates him from the window, on the other side of which raindrops have sequestered; staring out into the world beyond, where steel structures, post-Bauhaus, in the Dahlem Cube, support walls of hanging vines; where the cross beams divide the grey sky into rectangles, a man has, imminently in mind, memories of his son, singing. The son sings of the father experienced as one who never was a father to the son. The man has never heard this voice live, only as recorded, transmitted from cloud to device. He recognises, in the timbre of the voice, something of his own. This memory of sound is textured, for the man, with longing. There is no possibility of conversation.

Arm

In summer, the short sleeves of the blue school shirt expose too much of the boy's arms. On the right, the sleeve stops just above the keloid scar, sparking classmates' curiosity. The boy is not aware of the possibility of privacy, so does not question why the others need to know. Every time, he tells the story. To demonstrate the indentation where the scalpel broke dead skin and burst the abscess that formed in a burned compartment, the boy supinates the arm. He tells the little he remembers, and some of the rest that he's been told. When he was two, he climbed towards a bench top, pulled a jug of boiling water down. He does not remember screaming, searing pain or the weeks of delirium. In the face of further threat, his body recalls the mother's hand that held him as he teetered between worlds. Detachment, as he tells the story, will later serve him well, when in medical school, an arm is presented for anatomical dissection.

Window

A teenage boy stands before a mirror. He rubs vitamin cream into the scars that run in lines on the right side of his face. He has been told they will fade with time and that they fall in natural creases, but from photographs, he knows of the distortion that occurs each time he smiles. It grows, for him, each day, in its grotesquery. He remembers running down the stairs and out of the gym, to retrieve a ball. He remembers the sound of breaking, coming from far away, as his left hand, his right leg, his face breach the pane. He sees, on the cinema screen, when his eyes are shut, that someone's leg is open, exposing glistening bone. Blood spurts from an artery. The man that lays him down tears off his shirt to make a tourniquet. That man can see, behind the boy, the outline of a star. The boy has no awareness of the window.

Limb

Out of the brutish world,
a limb of the cassia tree
erupts with yellow flowers.

Releasing the window latch,
I reach for connection.
My grip will not relent,
tightened by fear my hold
will shrink this limb
back into winter.

I grasp it gently,
lest it retreat from my caress,
misapprehended as a hand
might be, about the throat,
intent to steal its breath.

Sheen

A pigeon fell and lay dead
on the red brick steps.
In a two season town,
the confused pigeon
came out too soon
in its spring plumage –
such a colourful sheen
on the dead bird's breast.

When the bird fell,
acridity hung in the air –
taking me back to the yard
where Father killed that chicken
we plucked in the shed –
like the stench of fowl giblets
mingled with the smell
left when forked lightning
strikes the sea strand,
leaving a glass flute
that glimmers.

Small Change

Tired as the old gods
of the corner of Queen and Edward,
I walk the streets of Brisbane
to that place where a stroke victim
flogging *The Telegraph*
once held his post,
shrapnel in his waist belt,
just enough for a bedsit,
back in nineteen eighty-two.

His revenant cries, '*Tele*!
Get your daily *Telegraph*!'

I pass his replacement,
abandoned in a wheelchair
with a fedora his only shelter
on that street corner,
grunting all day
and rattling his begging box.

I wander through the mall
where old soldiers
once were lovers.

1831 Boutique Hotel

Below my window,
double-glazed on second floor,
an oak hides the bobcat ripping asphalt
from the substrate of the road
the tree stubbornly penetrates.

The photos on the booking site
fail to show workers in reflector vests
digging up George Street,
raising hessian drapes on metal grills
outside the faux sandstone
Korean restaurant façade.

Under the sign with the silhouette
of a tow truck hauling a sedan,
a Kubato excavator blocks the view
of traffic into Chinatown.

No rollers smooth the road
where horse-drawn carriages
once clattered on cobblestones
and hotel windows opened
on a street where oaks
were full of birdsong
on Sydney sultry nights.
No Daikin air conditioners
hummed guests to sleep.

Boomer Stew

The '70s were times for culling kangaroos,
when Chum would keep the jump in your pooch:
98% kangaroo, 2% food colouring.

In 1992, the government declared the kangaroo
fit for human consumption, emu too:
national symbols became *cuisine nouvelle*. I'm worrying.

In the year 2042, the government declares the cull
on elderly. Too much drag on social security:
baby boomers in the stew. I'm scurrying!

After the Rain

What is the use of a Minister for Drought, after the rain,
when the fields spring up green and the land is renewed;
when all thirst is quenched and there's nothing to gain?

When rivers rise over their banks and farmers' pain
moves from parched earth to stock drowned in flood,
what is the use of a Minister for Drought, after the rain?

Party donors go dry while irrigation restrictions remain.
Now profit for mates is mourned as the great lost good,
when all thirst is quenched and there's nothing to gain.

When the aquifer rises and bursts through the drain,
when water flows everywhere, cheaper than blood,
what is the use of a Minister for Drought, after the rain?

Firefighters, forests and fauna, they all died in vain.
The cracked ground is deluged. It's no use to brood
when all thirst is quenched and there's nothing to gain.

While the country was burning it seemed quite insane
to approve a new coal mine, but need not be rued.
What use is a Minister for Drought, after the rain,
when all thirst is quenched and there's nothing to gain?

Magenta Shores

In this pale twilight,
we pass the beach houses
where retirees go to rest
on banksia-lined streets
of white architectural uniformity.

We brood as querulous misfits
in false community,
dreaming of an urban village
where the residents, drunk with poetry,
jam raucously on vintage instruments.

I push against a hedge to let
an old man in a golf cart
overtake us in the dusk
on the verge of the putting green
where managers and keepers
laid poisoned baits for rabbits.

On the edge of the resort,
we amble along the track
over the dunes to Tuggerah Beach.
We walk the line between foam and sand,
where kelp washes up as waves break,
then dump their load of silica
on the steep shelf.

In the afterglow
that follows sunset over the lake,
night stumbles and falls
until the moon rises,
then disappears behind a cloud.

Let's rest for a moment, you say.
I lower myself onto the sand
while you photograph the moon's demise.
I feel it in my joints. I seek
your assistance to rise.

Jazz Show in the Vines

We left home from Magenta, up through Norah Head,
driving through a black spot, lost the internet.
My thought train slid, as Coltrane dropped from Spotify,
down the sax keys of my mind, longing for my children
at the jazz show in the vines.

Children are the blue notes in the pentatonic line
as we leave the pier and pelicans at Budgewoi behind.
They ride the engine's murmur as we pass by Morriset,
saddening the timbre of the mortal instrument
that strains towards revival at the jazz show in the vines.

There's heartsink on the highway, crossing double lines,
dodging all the roadkill, traffic cops and fines.
We pull into the Caltex to refuel and refresh.
Fresh coffee and the love will bring us both
to the jazz show in the vines.

Pushing on through Cessnock, fibro shacks and wines,
take a left turn through Pokolbin, following the signs.
There'll be bubbles on arrival, brass arpeggios,
a chanteuse on the main stage, chatelaine by my side
proclaiming our arrival at the jazz show in the vines.

Benedictine On Ice

Put out the lights. I am sitting alone
playing blues in the dark tonight
with the louvres closed so the
golf club man five houses down
won't nail a cat to my door again.

Fingers walk back down the scale,
play back and forth all over the place,
right hand picking index and thumb,
as the Peavey amp blatts minor blues
through glass doors to the pond.

Index on the A note bass,
pinkie jumps three frets
to the flattened third, index to D,
then a flattened and a natural fifth,
index to seventh, ring to the octave A,
index down on the high string C,
then it's ring to the D and pinky down
on the octave flattened third again.

Between riffs, I sip Benedictine on ice
in the space made when my fingers tire
of pressing the bronze wound strings.
I scratch the callous against my nose,
check my blistered thumb,
lift the instrument to play,
then pause for Benedictine on ice.

Mingus' portrait on the wall winks.
Charles made egg nog
with bourbon and rum,
but my neighbour tells me, I'm not him.

Stevie Wonder plays fretless,
but I'm just bending in the dark
so my fingers know where to go
when I stare at the moon.

Maybe someday I'll learn to slap
so good I replace Morgan Jahnig
in Old Crow Medicine Show.

Then I'll know the intervals –
where to press without looking at the
ebony board where there are no frets.

I alternate blues minor and the
major scale, but I want to add
a flattened seventh when the ice melts
and the flavours run. I can taste
sweet spirit drip down my chin
as the moon rises over the pond.

The lights go out in the house
beyond where the golfing man
shoots in his sheets, as he will
when he's dead, if I'm loud enough
to disturb his grave. Maybe
he'll rise when Gabriel blows
his horn in time with my bass.

My fingers run over the frets,
pretending attempts at heptatonics
are not mistakes. Lack of obsession
and Linda May Han Ho
stand between me and a place
in the Pat Metheny Group.

I swing to the beat as the jumbo spruce
knocks Benedictine out of my glass
and the last of the ice all over the place.

Frogmouth Blood Moon Blues

Last night I met a frogmouth roosting on a wire.
My familiar frogmouth, roosting on that wire.
I stood in his moonshadow and met him eye to eye.

Fly away now frogmouth, fly far away from here.
Fly away now frogmouth, fly away from me.
Tomorrow I'll come follow wherever you lead.

A pair of tawny frogmouths fly away northwest.
That pair of tawny frogmouths flew away northwest.
I feel the heart of country like wingbeats in my breast.

Fly away now frogmouth, fly away from here.
Fly away now frogmouth, fly away from me.
I hear that country calling. I'll follow your lead.

A pair of tawny frogmouths flew beyond the moon.
I pray my mate will meet me at the blue blood moon.
Into the heart of country, we'll fly away there soon.

My Familiar Frogmouth

The smell of puppies drew the tawny frogmouth
swooping from the colony on Galloway's Hill.
Blinded by the lights, the bird flew across the deck

and through the French doors into the lounge
to crash against blinds, then dive the television set,
right itself and crash against the wall. Feathers fell.

I killed the lights, willed the bird to turn. It hung a moment,
then spun and flew, back towards the hill. My first encounter
with the night bird heralded confusion, a time to ride boundaries

between worlds, to cross regions in which distinctions
between dark and light disappeared. The sepia tones
of Siennese artists illuminated landscapes over which I flew,

umbre robes with arcane symbols falling from my shoulders
as dreams streamed out behind, then funnelled and fell
into the tornado. The fury restored my sense of chiaroscuro,

as would a collision of Urizen, riding his flaming disk,
with Vermeer's *Astronomer,* retiring late from night vision,
hoping to snatch a little sleep, his back stamped black.

Normative forces brought me crashing, much as solar flares
afflicted wax that fastened Icarus' feathers. After impact,
when I walked the Wynnum foreshore, the angry crone

appeared beneath the figs on the path by the playground
opposite the fish-and-chippery, she whom I tore when
I turned to chase the chimera of things the way they were.

Soon I found, that though I might, by strength of will,
jam my foot against the slamming door and force my way
back, the angel of that place had made a pact with Azrael,

who held his flaming sword to bar me from the house
where my heart sought to rest. It was then, on a walk
by the clump of trees at Norman Park, I met that bird again,

perched on a branch. I looked, and he looked back at me,
locked in atavistic recognition. The frogmouth and I were
now one spirit, as with all things, but more so, kindred.

There are no nights, even when the blood moon rises,
fecund over my horizon, on which I, feathered and transformed,
fly out my bedroom window, but my awareness travels

with the bird. In the night, I know that he will come to show me,
if I tune to the path of his flight and read it, just as I did
when I switched out that light and willed him to turn home.

Soon the stone that weighed me to the earth sank to my heart.
I left to find my way alone, wrenching filaments that might
be seen in fading light, the fibres of a child's forgiveness.

It was then that I asked Blake: If when I break from the marriage
of Heaven and Hell, those two lodges remain one in the other,
the other in one, one and the same, in the same place, one I cannot

break and then re-enter, then where does the nightjar fly?
Blake said I should ask Milton, who knew best of loss,
when Katherine died, who'd kept his talent live by scribing

when the poet's eyes went blind. And Milton said, You must
take your bird familiar out to heal, not lay that talent waste.
I took advice. I could not change my mind, so changed my place.

I made my bed where I could lift my feet just far enough
to cross the road, then moved to a place where jacaranda
bloomed each spring below my balcony, those purple flowers

that, in the cemetery, fall on my parents' graves. Walking from there,
I met two birds. The frogmouths roosted on a wire, communed with me,
then flew away, north-west. I followed on a flight to Longreach,

for an interview, saw brolgas dance, was offered earth to serve,
but nothing came from bones in that arid land, that mirage
that left me, dry with nothing but potential space, to travel south,

where black cockatoos and honey-eaters fed on banksias.
Black-tailed wallabies found me on the Redgum Trail
in Wyrrabalong National Park, and brush-tailed possums shrieked,

their eyes in torch light glowing red. Swallows came to nest
and feed their young in the adobe house they made on a security
sensor by the door. In spring, they circled and dived,

skimmed and played on the surface of a pond between the house
and the fairway that footed dunes beyond. Pelicans swooped on fish
in the shallows of the Tuggerah lakes and men cast rods

by caravan parks at The Entrance and Long Jetty, where there was
little industry, but the ice trade flourished. Wild surf dumped charcoal
from the fires at Wollombi and Lake Macquarie to wash up

on Tuggerah Beach. On the run from Pelican Point, the setting sun
glowed as a red disk, before it disappeared behind the pall
blowing from fires north-east of Sydney. While the nation burned,

I lived as alien servant to the surf culture, on Darkinjung land,
outside communion with the familiar. In this time, no frogmouths
came, until the death of my sister-in-law of the Kamilaroi mob.

I returned, for a school reunion, to Toowoomba, where she died
off country, far north of those plains of her birth. Even there,
in that drought-stricken land, I found fellowship and a sense

of the familiar. The names came back to me, attached to faces
of thirty-two children in the photograph of my primary class
of 1969, then matched to those of high school friends,

aged forty years on. At the cemetery, my parents lay as still
as they ever were beneath their plaques under the jacaranda.
That night, perched on a garden trellis, my sister-in-law's spirit

came as a frogmouth, then she flew away from the wire.
My grieving nieces told me their mother had been an owl,
but the totemic boobuk, the nightjar and the tawny frogmouth

were often confused, and feared by all except those that sought,
in spirit, to fly out to heal or to harm. I'd just been back to Brisbane
for another job interview. While waiting for an outcome,

my old neighbours, from the next apartment, sent me
photographs of tawny frogmouths roosting in the old familiar
jacaranda that fell below the balcony I'd left – three of them,

a nesting couple and their fledgling, now residing there,
singing their plaintive oom-oom-oom-oom, calling and willing
my spirit's winged return to the purple flowers of home.

Leaving

On my last office day, I clear shelves.
My name plate space reverts to blank.
I wait for you as afternoon wears on,
dressed in the jeans of serial collegial goodbyes.

Then packers at the beach house uplift everything
and drive the material evidence of our lives in boxes
to a domicile a few hours north. It's the end of May,
and bitter wind blows a diatribe against all landlords.

I hear breakers roll into the slope
of Tuggerah Beach and imagine
a humpback somewhere in the Tasman
bellowing as it breaches and blows.

About the Author

Andrew Leggett is an author and editor of poetry, fiction, song lyrics and interdisciplinary academic papers. Andrew has resided at various places in three Australian states, but now lives at Macksville, New South Wales, with his wife, Linda Kaarina. They collaborate musically to record as the Blood Moon Wailers. Andrew's writing is widely published in Australia and internationally. In addition to medical degrees and postgraduate qualifications in psychiatry and psychotherapy, he holds a master's degree in creative writing from the University of Queensland and a PhD from Griffith University. His two previously published collections of poetry, *Old Time Religion and Other Poems* (1998) and *Dark Husk of Beauty* (2006), were published by Interactive Press. He was editor of the *Australasian Journal of Psychotherapy* from 2006 to 2011. He is the current prose editor for *StylusLit*.

www.ingramcontent.com/pod-product-compliance
Lightning Source LLC
Chambersburg PA
CBHW062152100526
44589CB00014B/1797